Like Li-Po Laughing
at the Lonely Moon

Other books by Chuck Taylor:

Special thanks to Cheryl Clements, H. Palmer Hall, Janet McCann, Dave Oliphant, and Dave Parsons for their assistance.

Like Li-Po Laughing
at the Lonely Moon

a novella in verse by Chuck Taylor

Pecan Grove Press   San Antonio, Texas

The cover art is an artist's rendering of Li-Po
based upon a 13th century ink drawing

ISBN: 978-1-931247- 59-7

Pecan Grove Press
Box AL
1 Camino Santa Maria
San Antonio, TX 78228

*This book is dedicated to the great
Joseph Mallord William Turner,
English master painter.*

Contents

Like Li-Po Laughing at the Lonely Moon
1999

"For all life is a dream,
and dreams themselves are only dreams."
　　　　　　　　—*Pedro Calderon de la Barca*

for A

Like Li-Po Laughing at the Lonely Moon

The blues, in a small
upstairs club, she's said he can
play the blues—*Let me*

give you a chance—he's
always talking the blues, puts
blues in the shifting

poems he writes when he
sits in her quiet bar on
Tuesdays, downing a

draft, scribbling on damp
coasters in the moody dark.
A week from tonight

Vincent dreams he'll sing
in a club on Sixth downtown.
Soul from the country

he'll try to bring. He
dwells away from the city east
some seventy miles,

comes to town to see
daughters from his marriages:
Beth, a waitress at

Denny's, and Jane, the comic
at Ester's Follies.
His back yard faces

a slope you could call
a valley, fields once for farms,
now used for cattle

grazing, beef shipped to
Japan, though Vincent's rarely
seen any cattle.

Over the barb wire,
a few live oaks he's strolled to,
and a mile further

out, a small grove of
cottonwoods, and it looks like
some small apple trees

April blooming by
a quiet creek, while around
in front white wooden

houses across a
crooked gravel road and then
through a scrubby vacant lot,

a path that rambles
in a field that rises to
a low hill. How long

has he dreamed the old
vigil of shepherds free
of the valley of

sorrows? A year now
since his last split;
his new roommates, at

home rarely, a couple,
both commuters working in
computers, called him

on the phone and
offered, rent free, a tiny
back room after his

ad appeared in the
Sunday book section, "Poet,
poor, seeks Solitude".

To write at Grasmere
the husband says; *like Wordsworth,*
the wife adds, *or like*

the other poets of
nature we love, like Mary
Oliver or the

beat poet, Buddhist
Snyder. So Vincent spends his
somnolent days in

the back yard, in the
shade of a hackberry, or
out under the trees

in the field of dreams
where he's got a camera
and hopes to catch

the colors bleeding across
grass and sky, the gold at play
in the blue, gilding

for moments the land,
for eye—cyan to blue, the
pearling sustaining,

the sun moving on
the horizon like a blooming
red mountain rosebay.

Children play mornings
in the yard next door. He loves
the way the boy and

his sister flow on
bikes and bleed to light, and in
that bleed of light that

runs through time, Vincent
will see shadows move in the
blind of color and

then reappear, like
daughters who fade in and out.
And out in front, at

the break of day, the
sunrise umber will spill on
the hill across the

field and melt trees, spill
and flow over homes. Standing by
the chain link fence that

separates the yard
from neighbors, he has felt in
the evening's rise

of breeze and color,
the fence melting, sliding up
and away. Vincent

takes photos but the
image on the screen of the
digital doesn't

do what he knows in
the sliding hours, what he's come
to be, out here on

pocket change seeking
and dreaming, knowing no more
where the lines are drawn

or if such lines are
real. His playing the blues in
the city, that could

be a dream, though he's
got a guitar standing in
his room's corner. He'll

pick it up, strum a
few chords—Muddy Waters, Ma
Rainey, BB King,

Lighting Hopkins, Mance
Lipscomb, "I am a man. M—A—N."
Muddy died a month

after Vincent caught
his show in Austin. Did he
dream this time or is

it coming? Vincent
decides it's a dream, a song
of the good waters

of the mind—yes, of
course—unless pride's pricked the self,
his ego self, oh

the mortifying,
if he has to face a crowd
of Tuesday faces

in a bar on Sixth,
and fake that he can sing. A
single note he can't

read, not a single
note (true, many bluesmen could
not read), and he can't

sing a single song
all through—he's got a terror
sliver in his spine

but will not practice,
spending days in the lounge chair
out back, sipping sweet

Sangria wine, or
in front, watching the wind move
through the grasses like

invisible herds
of buffalo, watching the
shadows made by clouds

and the clouds' slow slide
off the horizon. Do the
spirits of the dead

ride the thunder
and flash of clouds to rain
down on us the blues?

Must be a dream, a
lawn chair dream outside
in the shifting wind

of sangria hours,
in the song of doves he can't
see and the yellow

hope of thistle blooms—
his watch says Tuesday and he
hasn't practiced, has

no desire to drive
the hard road to the city,
stays where he's at like

a house cat, scribbles,
reads, watches the colors that
come and go in the

sky, sleeps when the need,
wakes to cool nights to study
the moon's mute phases

and the splayed scope of
stars, hoping to slide around
the self to see the

face of God in the
great dark, to know the sleeper
who dreams us, or we

who dream the sleeper
who dreams us like colors on
shifting land or like

the stars in the great
carnival of the cosmos—
we who dream the one

who dreams us, we in
our dreaming like the lilies
of fields who toil not.

For food, Vincent's
making do with *raisons* and
dried plums and sun

flower seeds, carrots,
oranges and nuts, trying to
clean the system with

spring water from the
Fuji islands--tune himself
to the shifting truth.

Morning comes, and she
arrives at the house without
saying she's coming.

He remembers things
he dreamed, drawing a napkin
map, half inviting

her to come as a
thanks for listening—and here
she is as always

in t-shirt and jeans,
black hair clipped straight
at the shoulders,

calm and kind, not stressed
like you'd think from running a
club in your thirties.

Claire acts concerned
but he knows she's sad in her
small talk, lonely and

yearning for a road
to love. Vincent takes her down
the path around the

houses, up the low
hill where through mist and pollen
one can see far off

a silhouette on
the horizon, a hill by
the Brazos where the

Tonkawa performed
their rites and visions. As they
sit under small post

oaks, Vincent tells tales
of coyote and raven
and reads drafts of poems.

He's in shorts no shirt,
she pulls off her shirt for sun
and as in a dream

he's surprised by her
lovely breasts like sparrows
flitting—*I don't know*

a single blues song,
not all the way through, Claire. Can
barely strum ten chords

on a guitar. I
thought I would get some courage
going, fake my way

through a set, but no,
I'd melt, I'm not sure what's real
and what's not, I mean,

is this a dream, you
coming here or am I a
dream? Why would I try

to pass as a man
of the blues? I write, in the
lonely tower of

dreams, poems not made for
the stir of streets--like Li-Po
wine drunk under a

loony moon, tossing
songs, leaf by leaf, into a
stream. I know the tints

that come down the hill
we're on, the tints that are born
to burn, the colors—

the gods—that rise from
the valley, this breeze here of
silence in the dusk,

like Monet (Monet
you know) in his garden, the
painter on mornings

at Giverny, seeing the
haystacks' flow or the water
lilies' blend—I have

a friend in town, Gnome,
he calls himself, with a blue
line tattoos circling

his face. I sit in
his yard at a place called
Entropy—when I

come by to see him
under trees after his hard
day's labor, he laughs,

takes a deep slow drag
off his cigarette, and says—
if they're going to

burn it all down, they
ought to enjoy the colors,
they curse and sweat and

cry in the blues they
are bluing and don't enjoy
the old world burning.

Vincent tells of his
friend's despair in his judgments,
and doesn't draw a

line across what is
mind, what is real or form
or flowing. Claire smiles

and stands up and yawns.
She spins around, scanning the
horizon and puts

on her shirt; her breasts
are dreams of sunrises under
cotton—that's when he

knows she and the club,
the show he promised, could be
a dream or as real

as a dream and the
houses and fields, the low hill
behind the houses

and the path, the sun
rise and sun set and colors
coming and going,

the shadows of clouds
across wet fields, the trees and
the wind, that is no

dream in the dream while
he lives anyway, that's real,
that movement in the

valley of the shade
where he waits and walks and feels
no evil. *I made*

no woman happy,
Vincent says as they walk back
to her car and she

smiles and kisses him
on the cheek. *They left me, they
saw only sadness,*

they never saw joy—
but you see, Claire, you see where
the light shifts and meets

to make a beauty
that waits on all, Claire, for all
that is earth and us...?

Vincent's Li-Po

"Nature is commonplace. Imitation is more interesting."
—*Gertrude Stein*

Every Morning,

Every evening, water he pours
on the garden; every morning,
every evening, he walks
the rows bending to pull weeds,
pours water from his bucket
and listens to the plash of drops
on squash, watermelon, corn.
The eyes of the loved ones
greeting each and every day.

Li-Po Talks to Himself—

not to himself exactly but to a friend
who can't be there but who's loved
and missed. Li-Po talks hobbling the
rows weeding the garden. They are
such good buddies they leave things
out, speak in short hand phrases like
twins who have their own language.
Li-Po and ghost muttering with such
cranky joy and wizened animation—
never like the sullen city cafe
couples looking away, saying nothing.

Li-Po Writes

My friend, these men are without
honor. It is not safe to be in a
room with them. How do I know? I
have been in rooms where fathers
wept for their dead in faraway
wars. These men, parading in their
bright teeth, they should be beating
their heads in shame. You'd be better
off dancing with diseased whores
who ply an honest trade for money.

Li-Po and His Children

All those years apart, the
private ache in the heart.
I thought the pain never
would go away. Only the
moon saw on those roads,
only the moon relieved
my dark stumbling, the pound
of the head. A glass of
wine at a roadside inn,
then stepping into a
cool breeze with the crickets
singing, gave pause to a
lame and bitter howling.

Ah My Friend,

once again you invite
me to your house and once
again I hear all the
awful ways I wronged you.
Over your shoulder, out
the window, a martin runs
with song, and in the great
blue, spots of clouds ride west.
I'll take a glass of wine,
thank you. Soon enough, you
know, we will both be dead.

My Li-Po's Got a Dog

that beetles down
with him in the
bitten sheets

a dog who gets
him down the mountain
to fetch the wine

a dog who by
the campfire, with
raised ears big,

listens for the
slow broad walking
of the harvest moon

Li-Po Hope

Outside, boulders
rising in the mist
like grey whales
out of the sea,
but here, in this
public place, your
dark eyes in a
lovely dance from
the small gold
flecks in the
barely tea, all
the way up to
these yearning
moons of mine

Li-Po's

got his cash box
buried by a boulder
next to an oak
a morning's walk
from his bamboo hut

in the box are jewels,
copies of every poem
he floated
all those years
down river

Li-Po's Blessing

We spent half our lives at
the table, our mouths shut
but our teeth grinding. When
you left I hoped the bridge
over the great gorge would
sway and break, but you
walked to your home and I walked
here, where I fell in love
with the clouds silvered by
the moon and with my own singing.
I bless how absence all
these years made us happy.

Li-Po, Hep Cat,

wearing a trench coat,
a Boston Blackie hat
with a plaid scarf
blowing around the neck,
is rambling around the
country in a thirties'
car with a rumble seat.
He's due back by midnight,
in the blue mountains of
the eighth century, but right
now he's not thinking of
fairy godmothers or
pumpkins, he's sipping
from a silver vodka flask
and has an arm around
a moll he met in a bar.

Lament

Winter nights I slipped from
my hut and walked by the moon's
eye along your star glinted fields,
to knock on your door at the edge
of the village. I did not pound
hard for fear of dogs barking.
One bright night you let me in
to your fire, and then after a
month of nights hoping by your
door in the trying cold, I, poor
lover, plodded back through snow
and wind to my hut and sorrow.

All night I could not sleep,

All night this yearning for
the mountains, missing the rush
of winds through the pines.

Don't ask me of home or the
far away ones I carry in my heart.
We have our wine, friend, and
this half moon on the water.

We can sit on stones by the shore;
we can laugh to drown our sorrows.

Li-Po Joins AA

A man well into his prime
doesn't need a cup of wine.
A man embraced by solitude
swims a sea of plenitude.
A man drunk on the moon
lives inside a happy tune.
A man sane in his poems
knows the best of homes.

Li-Po's Fin

Fresh from the waters she rose, all
lambent and dewy, and he leaped from
his boat, tipsy in love, hoping to
hold her, to get her to promise never
to go again to the heavens, but hang
by his garden with the squash and the
melons where she and he could sign
drunken poems and laugh at the stars.

It was no moon, you fools, in the slow
waters of the Yangtze. It was my first
love, the teasing girl from up the road
whose hand a summer's day I clutched
behind my fathers' shed in a moment forever…

Note on Li-Po
(also Romanized as Li Tai-po, Li Bai, and others)

I love literary pranks and would love to claim that these poems are translations of a recently discovered manuscript by Li-Po that reveal another side of his genius. Sadly they are not. It is only the author, having fun with the persona of Li-Po.

Li-Po, China's most popular and perhaps greatest poet, lived from 701 to 762 AD. He grew up mostly in Szechwan and was given a position at the Hanlin Academy, which existed to provide scholarly expertise to the emperor, but the poet was exiled due to court intrigue. Li-Po spent much of his life wandering, was skilled as a swordsman, and married twice, once to the daughter of a former prime minister. He fled south during the rebellion of 755 and entered the service of Prince Lin. The prince's downfall sent him into a second exile, but he was eventually pardoned. Legend has it that Li-Po drowned, tipsy from wine, leaping into the Yangtze River, trying to embrace the moon.

8/12/05

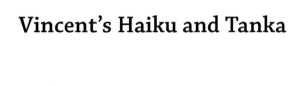

Vincent's Haiku and Tanka

for Claire

Haiku 1

This first frigid morn

Steam billows off this warm lake

Like peaks snow covered

Haiku 2

Small girl gathering

Off the green lawn a bouquet

of peacock feathers

Haiku 3

The rock overturned.

Underneath the rich damp earth

Pill bugs scurrying

Haiku 4

Small flock of sparrows

Capering between the church

And the woods nearby

Haiku 5

Steady yellow glow:

A lone firefly dying

In the wet, cut grass

Haiku 6

Spring: the snow fences

Along cracked county highways

Are bent and tired

Haiku 7

Walking by the church

A boy stops to piss on grass,

Sunlight in an arch.

Haiku 8

A cup of warm sake:

The rising mist caresses

Then flees the surface

Haiku 9/ Dishwasher

Stone white plates turned

Wings of Japanese motion by

Serene concert hands

Haiku 10

So it seems, marriage:

Oxen pulling a sharp star

Across the backyard

Tanka

As the wind stirs dark

post oak leaves bathing in the

sad November rain

in the dying light of dusk,

so leaves of love dark will stir

Tanka for Clair

A bright ardent moon

I just can't be, pushing through

Night clouds, confident

As ships plowing calm waters

Heading for ports of profit.

Nighthawk
(2006)

What atonement is there for blood spilt upon the earth?
—Aeschylus

for Will and James

Nighthawk

To walk down Congress
Avenue when most cars are
gone and the world has

gone silent, Vincent
from five to seven AM,
it's what he lives for,

to move down from the
state capital past the bridge
at Town Lake and see,

at sunrise, the bats
in a huge funnel cloud swing back
under the bridge from

their night's quiet feast
and slaughter. Here's beauty and
truth, truth and beauty,

all you know on earth,
and all you need to know, so
sleep your nights through. He

doesn't sleep; Vincent
haunts every night since his
oldest daughter Beth

refused to see or
speak to him. She's disappeared,
run off, since he fired

her from her job at
his store. He warned her—he told
her—if she again

disappeared for weeks
on drugs, didn't show up for
work, she'd be through, but

she didn't believe, of
course, thought her old man bluffing,
so she won't call back

when he calls. Doesn't
answer the door when he comes
by and rings the bell.

Something's broken. Two
years and no word. Something's not
working in his or

her soul, he's not sure
which. He can barely move these
days but in the night

the weight will lift, like
a dream he can slip down streets
and things acquire again

a taste of life, but
still the block of silence, words
can't be called from the

heart to the blood of
poems on paper, his soul, dead
or paralyzed, by

the grief of loss, by
the guilt for what he did, to
leave a child at five

years old, to be made
mad by passion, fleeing with
an older woman

he barely knew, like
painter Paul Gauguin fleeing
his family in

the grander service
of art, for Bohemian
Samoa, to laugh

like Li-Po at the
lonely moon. For that there can
be no atonement,

no plea to clear his
soul. For what he did there's long
days of guilt and grief,

whispered prayers at meals
and candles lit on church altars,
nights trolling empty

silent streets, sorrow
slowed by deprivation of
sleep, ebullient in

lost hope, in Spartan
girdling of loins in the high
of pain, *Hate me, child,*

hate me all you can
and all you want, give me due
coming, for the stones

laid down to blanket
your blameless innocence, stones
on one too young for

suffering...and yet,
Vincent's ashamed to say, he
claims consolations—

the gleam of headlamps
streaming on the black asphalt,
the wind sibilant

through the dark trees to
cool grief like sangria wine,
like the smooth of blues,

such sights and sounds make
room for dreams in a dream too
hard to dream a dream,

but Ruth's grief, the pain
seen in Beth's young mother, who
only wished that he

be what the world said
a man should be, these pains not
healed are the curse on

him, that's easiest
to say, the way it maims and
seems to kill, yet he,

well, he has no way
to wave away the curse that
burns her heart's stigma.

Does Beth walk the streets,
inner lanes of drugs that have
their beauties, that give

small consolation?
Vincent turns on Mary, named
for a slave. Mary,

slave of _____, the last
name after the Civil War
washed away and not

remembered by the
neighbors on the street today,
but Mary never

forgot, he's sure, and
Beth, she can't forget that who
she carries in this

not so civil war
is what she's been given to
carry and make her

blessing. Vincent's her
cross, her blood, her father. He,
by what mystery,

by what wavering
road, is the one of two who
gave the gift of life.

Vincent Goes Comic

(2008)

for Takako

Vincent Goes Comic

When the morning light
slid 'round through the mini blinds
Vincent slowly woke and

waited for the woman,
his agent, to wake. He knew
he needed to pee,

but instead slid his
hand down to the cold cement
under the bed to

check for dust to see
how well she did with household
chores in the loft she'd

bought. If she was not
the kind to obsess, she'd be
easier to love.

His fingers brushed on
something. He had to stretch to
reach his hand around

what felt to be a
book. He blew dust off, smiling,
and put the book on

his naked chest close
to his weak eyes and scanned
in the growing light

a poem. It was on
a tough who ran up behind
a tall thin boy to

shove him down, but the
boy bent down to tie his shoes,
and as if by magic,

the bully tumbled up
and over him, landing in
the playground dirt on

his back, getting the
wind slapped out of his lungs. In
bed the man thought, *This*

is not bad. It is
not stuck in the black tar
of relationships,

it's not Sylvia
calling her dad a Nazi
Panzer Man, dreaming

of gas and blue lips,
and then he noticed, on the
flyleaf, scribbled words

"To my wife and our
Love," in a hand that he knew
the author's sure hand.

Of course. Vincent shut
the book and saw on the back
a red circle smile

of a wine glass. He
set the book on the floor as
her eyes opened and

she saw him and seemed
surprised, and then smiled. He looked
back, his head nodding

up and down to say
yes and yes. He made a wink,
trying to think back

to a day in spring
when twelve in nineteen fifty
five he'd flipped by luck

this big kid on his
back who later became his
closest friend in town,

and now four months back,
his old friend left his wife of
twenty years. Kate was

their long-time agent,
reading always kindly his
rambling melancholy

poems that no one
liked to publish, so he'd
had to spend his life

on the telephone
selling cheap car insurance.
After dinner, wine

would write his verse while
he solitary listened
to his blues CDs.

He put his lips to
the sweet of her tousled salt
and pepper hair, sighing

and climbing out of
bed to pee, then smiled into
shifting morning light

that is the dream of
love. Love, he'd tried and failed
before, so always in the

bones, colors shifting
between dream and gloom. Four grown
children from other

loves they'd need to talk
to, to do more than placate,
in the name of love.

He is ancient now—
much easier in age's
tenderness, to love.

Recent Books from Pecan Grove Press

Davis, Glover. *Separate Lives.* 2007.
    ISBN: 1-931247-36-6 $12
Deibel, Tom. *Ellipses and Eclipses. 2007.*
    ISBN: 978-1-931247-40-5 $7
Dumitru, Cyra S. *remains.* 2008.
    ISBN: 978-1-931247-0 $15
Estess, Sybil Pittman. *Labyrinth.* 2007
    ISBN: 978-1-931247-41-2 $15
Hopes, David Brendan. *A Dream of Adonis.* 2008.
    ISBN: 978-1-931247-42-9 $15
Jennings, Rachel. *Elijah's Farm.* 2008.
    ISBN: 978-1-931247-51-1 $17
Kittell, Linda. *The Helga Pictures.* 2008.
    ISBN: 978-1-931247-55-9 $9
Lazar, David. *Powder Town.* 2008.
    ISBN: 978-1-931247-52-8 $17
LeCoeur, Jo. *Medicine Woods.* 2008.
    ISBN: 978-931247-45-0 $8
McVay, Gwyn. *Ordinary Beans.* 2007.
    ISBN: 978-1-931247-39-9 $15
Morton, Colin. *The Local Cluster..* 2008.
    ISBN: 978-1-931247-54-2
Myers, Tim. *That Mass at Which the Tonguie Is Celebrant.* 2008
    ISBN: 978-931247-43-6 $8
Peckham, Joel B. *the heat of what comes.* 2008.
    ISBN: 978-1-931247-49-8 $15
Roberts, Suzanne. *Nothing to You.* 2008.
    ISBN: 978-1-931247-46-7 $15
Roe, Margie McCreless. *Call and Response.* 2008.
    ISBN: 978-1-931247-56-7 $15
Soina, Vincent. *Outer Borough.* 2008.
    ISBN: 978-1-931247-53-5. $17
Taylor, David. *Praying Up the Sun.* 2008.
    ISBN: 978-1-931247-50-4 $17
Willis, Paul. *Visiting Home.* 2008.
    ISBN: 978-1-931247-47-4 $17
Wayne, Jane O. *From the Nightstand.* 2007.
    ISBN: 1-931247-38-2 $15
Whitbread, Thomas. *The Structures Minds Erect.* 2007.
    ISBN: 978-1-931247-24-2 $15
White, Anthony Russell. *These Bones Remember.* 2008.
    ISBN: 978-1-931247-32-0 $8

For a complete listing of Pecan Grove Press titles,
please visit our website at *http://library.stmarytx.edu/pgpress*